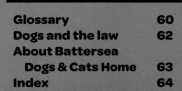

Introduction: Owning a dog

Dogs have lived alongside people for thousands of years, but they are more than just our pets. Dogs are our trusty companions, lively playmates and ever-faithful friends. Owning a dog is a hugely enjoyable experience. It is also a big commitment. It means being responsible for the dog's health, safety and happiness for the whole of his life.

Before getting a dog, ask yourself the following questions. If the answer to any of them is "no", then you're probably not ready for a dog. If your answer is always "yes", then read on to learn how to care for your dog in the best possible way.

Will I walk him every day?

Dogs need exercise every single day, no matter what. Even when it's raining, snowing, or there's something great on TV.

Will I care for him?

Dogs need to be fed, groomed and taken to the vet when they are sick. They also need people to clean up their poo!

Will he have company?

Dogs are social animals and get lonely if left alone. It's not fair to leave a dog by himself all day. There must be someone at home to look after him.

**Battersea
Dogs & Cats Home**

Caring for
DOGS
and PUPPIES

Ben Hubbard

W
FRANKLIN WATTS

This edition published in 2015
by Franklin Watts

Franklin Watts
338 Euston Road
London NW1 3BH

Franklin Watts Australia
Level 17/207 Kent Street
Sydney, NSW 2000

Produced under licence from Battersea Dogs
Home Ltd. ® Battersea Dogs & Cats Home

Royalties from the sale of this book go
towards supporting the work of Battersea
Dogs & Cats Home (Registered charity no
206394)

Series editor: Sarah Peutrill
Series designer: Matt Lilly
Picture researcher: Diana Morris
Photographs: Clint Singh,
unless otherwise stated
Illustrations: Jason Chapman

The Author and Publisher would like to thank
the staff of Battersea Dogs & Cats Home for
their guidance with this book.

Picture credits:
Illustrations © Jason Chapman 2014
Photographs © Clint Images/Battersea Dogs
& Cats Home 2014, unless otherwise stated
(see page 64)

Dewey number: 636.7'083
ISBN: 978 1 4451 2779 8

Printed in China

Franklin Watts is a division of Hachette
Children's Books,
an Hachette UK company.

www.hachette.co.uk

Contents

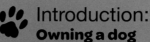

Introduction:

Chapter 1:
Choosing your dog

Chapter 2:
Bringing your dog home

Chapter 3:
Food and feeding

Will I have space?

Dogs need somewhere to sleep and a place outside to go to the toilet. A small puppy also takes up more room when he grows into a bigger, adult dog.

Will I be patient?

Dogs have to be housetrained and taught how to behave well. Teaching your dog takes many hours and is a vital part of having a happy life together.

Will the answer to these things be "yes" for 12 years or more?

This is the average length of a dog's life. Some dogs can even live to over 20! Owning a dog is an exciting and rewarding adventure. But you have to be prepared to go the distance.

Top tip!

Get your whole family involved in answering these questions. You'll need their help with your dog too!

Chapter 1: Choosing your dog

🐾 A big decision

There is a lot to think about when choosing a pet dog. Would you like a puppy or an adult? A male or a female? Is a pure-breed, cross-breed, or Mongrel best? As you learn about the different types of dog, think about which one would best fit into your family life and home.

Puppy or adult?

Puppies are cute, but they are also a lot of work. During the first few months they need to be fed and taken out to the toilet several times a day. Puppies have to be housetrained and taught how to behave, but often make a mess. Adult dogs that have been taught the basics are less work to begin with. However, some dogs may have habits that you'd like to change.

All puppies need constant care to begin with.

Both male and female dogs make equally good pets.

Male or female?

Male and female dogs that have been neutered are very similar. Neutering is a common operation to stop dogs producing puppies (see pages 52–53). Unneutered males often roam, looking for females. Unneutered females have to be kept inside when they are 'in season' (when they are ready to become pregnant). But once neutered, there are few differences between a male and female dog.

Pure-breed, cross-breed or Mongrel?

Dogs have developed over thousands of years into a number of different breeds and types. Today, we group them as pure-breeds, cross-breeds and Mongrels. Pure-bred dogs are those with parents of the same breed. Cross-bred dogs have parents from different breeds. Mongrels come from a mixture of breeds. With a pure-bred puppy, you will know what sized adult he will become and roughly what his character traits are. With a cross-bred and Mongrel dog there is more guesswork, but learning his character traits can also be great fun. This is also true of every dog. Whether you have a cross-breed, Mongrel or pure-breed, all dogs are individuals with unique personalities to discover.

Pure-bred dogs look just like their breed.

Cross-bred dogs are a mixture of two breeds.

Mongrels come from lots of different breeds.

Top tip!

Try and meet as many dogs as you can before choosing one. Dog events are a great place to see different dogs and talk to their owners.

Ask the expert!

Q

How many dog breeds are there?

A

The UK Kennel Club recognises 210 dog breeds in the United Kingdom.

🐾 Dog groups

There are seven main pure-breed dog groups. The dogs within each group were bred for a particular purpose or job. Knowing the different groups can help you choose a dog which matches your lifestyle. A working dog bred for herding sheep may not suit a small city flat, for example.

Hounds

Hounds were bred to hunt and are friendly with both humans and other dogs. There are two hound types: sight hounds and scent hounds. Sight hounds can sometimes be tempted to chase moving things, and scent hounds get easily distracted by different smells.

The Afghan Hound loves chasing and needs regular grooming.

Gundogs

Gundogs were bred to flush-out and fetch game birds for hunters. There are four gundog types: Retrievers, Spaniels, Setters, and HPRs (Hunt, Point and Retrieve). Gundogs are sociable, playful and easy to train.

The Pointer is affectionate, active and has an amazing sense of smell.

Terriers

Terriers are dogs bred to catch rats, rabbits and other countryside pests. They are full of energy, have big personalities, and can often be excitable.

The Scottish Terrier is a proud and sometimes stubborn character.

Utility dogs

Utility dogs are a mixture of different dogs bred for a range of roles. Today, they are most often kept as pets. Each breed should be researched individually.

The Poodle is famous for being intelligent, playful and affectionate.

Pastoral

Pastoral dogs were bred to herd and protect sheep and cattle. They are alert, hard working and need loads of exercise. Herding dogs such as collies are very bright and learn quickly.

Old English Sheepdogs are large, energetic dogs with lots of hair!

Working dogs

Workings dogs were bred to help humans with activities such as search and rescue operations. They tend to be keen and need a lot of exercise.

The Siberian Husky was bred to pull sleds and needs to be walked for several miles a day.

Toy dogs

Toy dogs make up a mixture of small breeds, some of which were bred as pets and companions. Each breed should be researched individually. Toy breeds are usually friendly and love attention, and owners should take care to treat them as dogs not toys.

The Pomeranian is a lively dog with a high-pitched bark.

🐾 Popular breeds

When choosing a pure-bred dog, it is helpful to know about the breed's size, the care he will need, and his character traits. A character trait is a typical behaviour. Knowing the different breeds will also help you identify certain character traits in cross-breeds and Mongrels. The following table shows some of the most popular dog breeds.

Breed		Group	Size
	Border Collie	**Pastoral:** bred for herding sheep.	**Medium:** 46–54cm high.
	English Springer Spaniel	**Gundog:** bred for flushing out game.	**Medium:** 46–48cm high.
	Akita	**Utility:** bred for hunting and guarding.	**Large:** 61–71cm high.
	Labrador Retriever	**Gundog:** bred for retrieving.	**Large:** 55–57cm high.
	Jack Russell Terrier	**Terrier:** bred for hunting small animals.	**Small:** 23–26cm high.
	Greyhound	**Hound:** bred for hunting.	**Large:** 69–76cm high.
	German Shepherd	**Pastoral:** bred for herding.	**Large:** 58–63cm high.

Traits	Care needed
Intelligent, energetic and loves games.	Lots of physical and mental stimulation to prevent bad habits forming.
Quick to learn, energetic and a good swimmer.	Lots of long walks and play or may become mischievous.
Confident, loyal and reserved in nature.	Long walks and lots of socialisation as a puppy.
Good natured, patient, prone to weight gain and a good swimmer.	Lots of toys to chase and chew, and careful control of his diet as he can become greedy with food.
Confident, energetic and easily excited.	Lots of mental stimulation, but watch around small animals and people he doesn't know.
Good natured, affectionate and likes to chase.	You may have to keep on a lead when walking and watch he doesn't chase after small animals.
Loyal, strong, loves to chase.	Lots of mental and physical stimulation and toy-chasing games.

Breed		Group	Size
	English Cocker Spaniel	**Gundog:** bred for flushing out game and retrieving.	**Medium:** 38–41cm high.
	Golden Retriever	**Gundog:** bred for retrieving game.	**Large:** 51–61cm high.
	Rottweiler	**Working dog:** bred as a guard dog.	**Large:** 58–69cm high.
	Pug	**Toy:** bred as a pet.	**Small:** 25–28cm high.
	Staffordshire Bull Terrier	**Terrier:** bred for bull baiting.	**Medium:** 43–48cm high.
	Boxer	**Working dog:** bred for hunting.	**Large:** 53–63cm high.
	Doberman	**Working dog:** bred for guarding people.	**Large:** 65–69cm high.
	Siberian Husky	**Working dog:** bred for sled-pulling.	**Large:** 51-60cm high.
	Cavalier King Charles Spaniel	**Toy:** bred as a pet.	**Small:** 31–33cm high.

Traits	Care needed
Gentle, friendly, active and playful.	Lots of exercise, training and catch-and-retrieve games.
Powerful, loyal and affectionate. Loves water.	Loves games with toys and his coat needs lots of grooming.
Friendly, alert, loyal.	Lots of training and exercise, and socialisation as a puppy.
Loyal, confident and affectionate, but can get overexcited.	Wrinkles on the face need to be kept clean to protect against infection. Prone to breathing problems.
Fun-loving, protective and stubborn.	Needs lots of training to learn manners and early socialisation with other dogs.
Strong, smart and naturally protective.	Games, long walks and training to prevent him from jumping up.
Playful, independent and loves to run.	Socialisation from an early age to develop into a happy, confident dog.
Lively, independent and loves to run.	May have to be kept on a lead at times to stop him chasing small animals.
Devoted, good-natured and happy to keep human laps warm.	Play, exercise and regular grooming to keep his coat tidy.

🐾 Where to pick your pet

The best place to find a dog is from a rescue centre or a breeder. Dogs from respectable rescue centres will be vaccinated, microchipped and well cared for. The same should be expected from a good dog breeder. Make sure you do lots of research and are happy with the place and people you are getting him from.

Breeders

Always visit the puppies in a breeder's home before buying one. The home should be a family environment similar to yours. The mother and puppies should be calm, happy, confident and eager to say hello. Ask the breeder if the puppies have been vaccinated and treated for worms and parasites. Spend a good amount of time with a puppy before deciding he is the one for you.

Puppy checklist

Before buying a puppy, make sure he:

- 🐾 Is seven weeks of age, or older.
- 🐾 Has a healthy coat, clear eyes and moves around easily.
- 🐾 Has been raised in the same place he was born.
- 🐾 Has vaccination documents stamped by a vet.
- 🐾 Has a pure-breed certificate (if a pure-breed) and has had all the medical tests for the breed.

Rescue dog

Rescue centres, such as Battersea Dogs & Cats Home, rehome thousands of dogs every year. Rehoming is a wonderful way to give a new start to a dog who is unwanted or without an owner. Rescue dogs are a mix of pure-breeds, cross-breeds and Mongrels. The staff at a rescue centre will interview you to find the dog that is the best fit. Then you'll be able to spend time with the dog to see if you like each other.

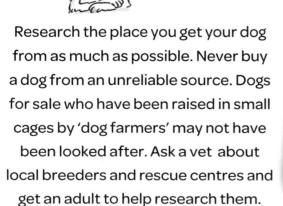

Top tip!

Research the place you get your dog from as much as possible. Never buy a dog from an unreliable source. Dogs for sale who have been raised in small cages by 'dog farmers' may not have been looked after. Ask a vet about local breeders and rescue centres and get an adult to help research them.

Chapter 2: Bringing your dog home

🐾 Get prepared

Make sure your home is ready for your new dog before he arrives. You will need a dog bed, toys, food, a food and water dish, a collar, lead and ID tag, and a pet carrier to transport him. It's also important to make your home and garden safe for your new pet.

A dog bed

Your dog will need a bed that he gets used to sleeping in every night. Make sure you buy a strong bed that your dog can't chew-up or destroy. A machine-washable dog blanket will keep the bed soft. Place the bed somewhere out of the way, such as a quiet kitchen corner, so your dog can have some private space.

Toys

Specially-made dog toys are a great way of keeping your dog entertained, while giving him something to chew on. Toys should be chewable and not sharp or small enough to swallow. Toys that squeak are a particular favourite, as are rubber 'Kongs®' that have hidden treats inside.

A dog-proof home

Dogs love to explore, chew and investigate anything new. Small items that could choke your dog are the most dangerous for him. It's best to keep everything out of reach, including: electrical cords, shoes, items on coffee tables and pot plants.

Dog identity

The law says your dog must wear a collar with an ID tag so your family can be contacted if he gets lost. When attaching a collar, make sure you can fit two fingers between the collar and your dog's neck. Keep checking the collar is not too tight, especially if it is on a growing puppy. Your dog should also be microchipped. This involves inserting a microchip containing a special reference number into the scruff of a dog's neck. The microchip can be scanned to access the owner's details from a database.

Top tip! Make sure you keep your dog's microchip details up to date.

Ask the expert!

Q

Can dogs open drawers and cupboards?

A

Yes, and they can hurt themselves on whatever is inside. Your parents may want to attach child protection locks to low-level drawers and cupboards. Anything dangerous or poisonous must always be kept out of a dog's reach.

🐾 The first day

Bringing your new dog home is the exciting moment you've been waiting for. But for your dog, the strange sights and smells in its new home can be a bit scary. It is up to you to give your dog a calm and comforting first day.

When you and your parents introduce your dog to his new home, the main thing is to let him settle in gently. First, take your dog outside in case he needs to go to the toilet. If he does, make sure to praise him. Then take your dog into the room where he'll spend the first few days. This should also be where his bed, food and water dishes are. Let him explore, have a sniff around, and play with his toys if he wants. If your dog settles down to sleep, let him do so.

Becoming buddies

Help your new best friend get to know you by kneeling beside him and letting him sniff your hand. Let your dog approach you and always have a toy ready to play with. Talk to your dog in a gentle voice and say his name when you stroke him so he gets used to hearing it. Stroke your dog along his back and chest but avoid touching his head and tail, which most dogs dislike.

Top tip!

Never shout at your dog, or you will make him scared of you.

Ask the expert!

Q

Where should my puppy go to the toilet?

A

Take your puppy outside regularly to go to the toilet and praise him when he does so (see pages 44–45 for housetraining).

🐾 Meeting the family

The rest of your family will be waiting excitedly to welcome your new pet. It won't take long for them all to become great friends. But to start with, meeting lots of new people may make your dog nervous. Make sure everyone in your family knows some basic dog safety before being introduced.

When first meeting your dog, family members should sit quietly and let the dog come up to them to say hello, rather than crowding around him. It is best if the dog is not picked up unnecessarily.

Puppies especially are not used to being picked up, and being grabbed suddenly can frighten them. Small children can get overexcited around dogs and should never be left with a dog without an adult present. To start with, your new dog should be allowed plenty of space and a calm, quiet environment so he can get used to his new family.

Doggy dos and don'ts

Show your whole family these safety tips, so everyone knows how to look after your dog.

🐾 Always stay calm and remember that staring may scare your dog.

🐾 Don't make any sudden movements or loud noises.

🐾 Don't kiss or hug your dog, or he may feel worried.

🐾 Call your dog, rather than pick him up. This makes sure he wants to spend time with you.

🐾 Leave your dog alone when he is eating, or he may feel he has to protect the food.

🐾 Play games with your dog, such as chase and retrieve.

🐾 Stop playing a game if your dog gets overexcited, or starts to bite. This helps him learn to behave well when you play.

🐾 Make sure you wash your hands after touching your dog and don't let him lick your face.

Top tip!

Always let your dog move away from you if he wants to, or he may become scared.

Ask the expert!

Q

Is it ok to wake my sleeping dog?

A

No. You should always leave your dog alone while he is sleeping.

🐾 Meeting other pets

Introducing a new dog to your existing pets should be taken slowly and gently. Keep the first few meetings short, so the animals have time to get used to each other. Make sure both your pets feel equally loved and looked after.

Introducing your dog

Together with two adults, introduce your dogs somewhere outside the home such as your garden. Having a play session with each dog first helps them to keep calm.

1 Start the dogs apart from each other, with both on a loose lead held by an adult.

2 If they seem relaxed, let the dogs go up and greet each other.

3 If they stay relaxed, let them continue getting to know each other.

4 If both dogs are still at ease, they can be taken off their leads and let inside together.

5 To start with, keep your dogs in different rooms when nobody is at home and feed them in separate places. Put most of your dog toys out of sight for the first few days too.

Introducing your cat

Cats can be of great interest to a dog as an animal to chase. The best way to avoid this is to teach your dog that the fun is elsewhere.

1 Together with an adult, put your dog on a lead and take him into a room that your cat is in.

2 Keep your dog at the furthest distance from your cat and whenever he seems interested in her, stop paying attention to him.

3 If he tries to chase the cat, restrain him with the lead.

4 Whenever your dog is ignoring the cat, praise him.

5 Your cat might come up to your dog, watch from a distance, or leave the room. Keep the introduction sessions short and use a long lead until you're confident your dog won't chase your cat.

6 Make sure the cat has plenty of escape routes and high hiding places to jump up to. A baby gate on a doorway can provide an easy exit for your cat, but stops your dog following.

Top Tip!

Rubbing rags on your new dog and leaving them around the house will help your other pets get used to his smell.

🐾 Settling in

During the first few weeks, it is important to create a routine for your new dog. This will help you organise his care and provide some order in his life. A dog's day includes feeding, exercising and resting, and should fit in with your normal family life.

Your dog should be let out to go to the toilet first thing in the morning and fed (see pages 26–27 for feeding). Once you have given your dog his food, step away and don't pester him until he's finished. Puppies will need more looking after than adult dogs, including more meals, more play periods, more rest and more toilet breaks. Somebody will need to be at home during the day to look after your dog and let him out.

Playpen

Puppies need human care throughout the day. When you can't watch him, a playpen can provide a safe space which your puppy can't escape from. A playpen should be big enough for your puppy to move around in and also fit his bed and food and water dishes.

Only use a playpen for a short period and never as a prison for a naughty puppy. When you are around, leave the door open so your puppy can wander in and out. When your puppy starts to choose to settle in the playpen you can close the door for short periods of time, gradually building it up. Only let your puppy out when you are ready and not because he is barking or whining as this teaches him to bark to be let out!

Top tip!

Leave a filled hot water bottle wrapped in a blanket in your dog's bed to comfort him at night. Make sure the water is not too hot and that he has a cool area to sleep in too. A ticking clock by your dog's bed can also make him feel less lonely as it mimics the heartbeat of his mum and littermates.

Sleeping dogs

At bedtime, give your dog a treat on his bed, turn out the lights and leave the room. Ignore your dog if he whines or scratches at your door in the night, or he will know he can get your attention this way.

Chapter 3: Food and feeding

🐾 A balanced diet

Dogs love to eat and most will chomp down any food they are given. It is your job to feed your dog with a balanced diet that provides everything he needs. This means a regular mix of all the food groups: protein, carbohydrates, fats, fibre, minerals and vitamins. Provide fresh water for your dog and make sure to clean his bowl every day.

Types of food

You can feed your dog dried food, canned food or home-prepared food. Dried or canned foods labelled 'complete' should contain the right mix of food groups to meet your dog's needs. Many dog owners stick to the 'complete' foods found at the supermarket for most of their dog's life.

Changing needs

Sometimes your dog's nutritional needs will change. This happens as your dog ages and if he is overweight, unwell or lacking in a particular food group. When these things take place, your vet will be able to tell you which food groups he needs more of. There is often a 'complete' food available that takes care of these changing needs.

Food groups

Protein
Found in meat, fish and eggs, protein is essential for growth. Puppies need lots of protein.

Carbohydrates
Dog biscuits, biscuit meal and cooked rice contain carbohydrates. Carbohydrates provide energy.

Fat
Milk and protein foods are the main sources of fat. Fat provides even more energy than carbohydrates, but too much turns into body fat.

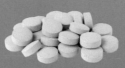

Vitamins and minerals
Given as supplement tablets, vitamins and minerals help your dog to resist illness and are good for his overall health.

Fibre
Vegetables, rice and biscuit meal are all sources of fibre, which helps your dog's digestion.

Water
Provide a bowl of fresh water for your dog.

Treats
You can use food from your dog's daily food allowance for treats, or purchase specially-made dog treats.

 A dog's dinner

Young puppies need several meals a day to give them energy and help them grow. As your dog gets older the amount of food he needs will change. It is important to always give your dog the correct amount of food and not overfeed him.

How much?

The amount you feed your dog depends on his age, breed and weight. Young puppies should be fed three or four meals per day until they are around four to six months old.

As your dog grows, it's important to weigh him regularly. To do this, hold him as you stand on some bathroom scales. Simply subtract your own weight from the total to find out how much your dog weighs. Then, check the guidelines on your chosen dog food to work out how much he should be fed. Often it is helpful to pop in and weigh your dog on your vet's special dog scales. If you are unsure about your dog's food allowance this can also be discussed with the vet.

Snacks and titbits

As tempting as it may be, it is best not to give your dog scraps or titbits of food during your meal times. Dogs begging for food should be discouraged and snacks outside your dog's meal times are bad for his health. Even small morsels of human food have far more calories than a dog needs, and snacks and titbits will cause him to become overweight. For example, half a tin of tuna is the same for a dog as a person eating a fish and chip dinner. One small sausage for a dog is the same as a large steak for a person.

Top tip!

Keep out of the way while your dog eats. Remove his food bowl if he hasn't eaten after 20 minutes. Heavy bowls or bowls with a rubber rim are best to stop them moving around.

Ask the expert!

Q

Can my dog have sweet food like chocolate?

A No. Sweet foods are not good for dogs. Chocolate, in particular, is poisonous to dogs.

Chapter 4: Play and exercise

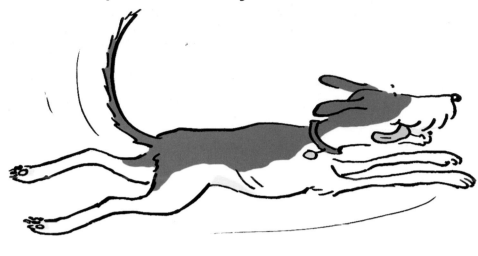

🐾 Building trust

Playing games with your dog is an essential part of your life together. Play provides your dog with exercise, keeps his mind active and helps him relax. It also creates a close bond between you. Through play, your dog will learn to trust you and listen to your instructions.

Keep it fun

Games have to be fun to stop your dog becoming bored. The more fun you have with your dog, the more he will want to please you and do what you say. In this way, games help train your dog. If your dog bites, jumps up or gets too over-excited, end the game immediately and walk away. Your dog will quickly learn that this behaviour will stop him from having fun! Different breeds of dog prefer different games, but there are two that most enjoy: tug of war, and chase and retrieve. Make sure you use the correct toy for each game, as objects such as sticks can splinter and injure your dog.

Tug of war

This is a good inside game to stop your puppy 'mouthing', which means biting hands and clothes. A large toy that keeps your hands far away from the dog's mouth is perfect for this game.

1 Wriggle the toy around on the ground in front of your dog to get him interested.

2 Let your dog bite down on the toy, while holding onto it.

3 Enjoy a fun game of tug of war!

4 If your dog loosens his grip on the toy and lets you take it, praise him.

Top tip!

Put some of your dog's toys away for a while after play sessions. This means your dog won't get bored with them.

Ask the expert!

Q

How long should I play with my dog for?

A

Lots of short sessions of a few minutes each are better than one long play session.

🐾 Outside play

Outside games should be exciting, entertaining and enjoyable for you and your dog. Ideally, your dog will be so involved in the game that he is not interested in anything else.

Chase and retrieve

This is a popular game for you, your dog, and an adult friend or family member. Use two interesting toys for the game, such as balls that squeak.

1 Show your dog the toy and get him interested in it. Your friend will keep him in one place by holding onto his collar.

2 Bounce or throw the toy along the ground and call "fetch it!". As you call "fetch it", your friend should release your dog.

3 When your dog picks up the toy, run away in the opposite direction so he chases you.

4 After a while, let your dog catch you up and give him lots of praise.

5 When your dog lets go of the toy, throw the second toy so he chases after that one. You can continue in this way until you've both had enough!

Top tip!

Always have a backup toy with you when you're playing with your dog. That way you can swap it for the one your dog has in his mouth.

6 When your dog gets good at playing chase and retrieve you can change the rules by hiding a toy instead of throwing it. Point in the direction of the toy as you call "fetch it" and see if your dog can find it.

Ask the expert!

Q

When can I take my dog out into the world beyond my own house and garden?

A

You can take your dog safely into the outside world after he has had the relevant vaccination injections and been given the 'all clear' by your vet (see pages 52–53).

Chapter 5: Understanding your dog

🐾 Dog poses

Dogs 'speak to you' through their body language, facial expressions and vocal sounds. This is why your dog always looks at your body language before trying to understand what you are saying. By recognising your dog's body language, you will be better able to understand what he is saying to you.

Happy, scared or angry?

There are three important body language poses that every dog owner should know. These are your dog's way of telling you he is happy, scared or angry. A happy dog is showing you it is ok for you to approach him. An angry dog is showing you that he needs some space. The following pages will explain what the three body language poses look like, and how best to behave around them.

Happy

A happy dog has soft eyes, slightly pulled-back ears and a wagging tail. His body will be relaxed, his weight balanced across all four feet and his mouth open. A happy and relaxed dog can sometimes get overexcited to see you. He might jump up or wriggle around a lot. If your dog gets too overexcited you can help calm him down by offering a toy to hold in his mouth. Make sure you stay calm yourself! Don't run around, wave your arms, or make too much noise, as this will excite your dog even more.

Playbow

A happy and playful dog often gets into a 'playbow' pose, with his front end on the ground and his back end in the air. A playbow pose means "I'm ready for fun!"

Top tip!

When dogs stare and show their teeth it is to tell another dog to "back off". But humans do this to smile. It may take your puppy a while to recognise the difference.

Sending a signal

When dogs become scared or angry they are not relaxed. This means you need to be extra careful around them. An angry dog is telling you to back off, while a scared dog needs you to be calm and careful around him.

Scared

A scared dog tucks his tail between his legs, flattens his ears against his head and tries to look small. He may have large eyes, an arched back and a trembling body. He may also pant or bark. If your dog is scared it's important to stay calm and quiet around him. Don't stare, as this can worry him even more. Instead, talk to your dog in a quiet, soothing voice. If he comes up to you, avoid touching him, as this may cause panic. It's best to let a scared dog settle down in his own time.

Top tip!

You should have an adult with you when you are around any dog – even your own.

Angry

An angry dog will have his tail in the air, a stiff body, and his ears pointing forward. His mouth will be drawn back in a snarl to expose his teeth, and he may growl and bark. His eyes will be narrow and he will maintain eye contact. There are different reasons for your dog becoming angry. You may have done something that has given him a fright. Or he may be protecting something he doesn't want you to have.

If your dog becomes angry you should:

1 Stand still.

2 Look away.

3 Let go of anything you are holding that your dog may want.

Ask the expert!

Q

How can I make sure my puppy becomes a friendly adult dog?

A

To do this your puppy needs to socialise with lots of different people and dogs, so he is relaxed around them as he gets older (see pages 42–43 for socialisation).

🐾 Being a dog

Dogs are descended from wolves and their senses are designed to help them survive in the wild. By knowing how a dog's senses work, you will be able to better understand what it is like to be a dog. This will help you see things from your own dog's point of view.

Smell

Smell is a dog's main sense. While a human investigates with his eyes, a dog uses his nose. A dog's sense of smell is many times better than our own. Dogs can smell where a person has walked days after they have passed. They can sniff out someone trapped under metres of snow. They can even often smell their owner before seeing them. So when your dog is sniffing about, what he is doing is collecting information about the world around him.

Hearing

Dogs have an amazing sense of hearing. They can hear things many times further away than humans. They can hear high frequency noises we cannot, such as dog whistles and squeaking rodents. They can even swivel their ears in different directions to hear things more clearly. When you see your dog prick up his ears, he has probably heard something that you have not. For this reason, noises like fireworks and trains sound very loud to a dog indeed!

Sight

Dogs do not see as well as humans do. Objects appear more blurry to dogs and they do not see the same range of colours we do. However, dogs can see better than humans in dim light, such as at dawn and dusk. They are also better at seeing moving objects than us. This is why a dog can jump at exactly the right moment to catch a ball travelling at top speed.

Watching you

Dogs communicate through body language and your dog will watch you more than you think. This is how your dog knows you are getting ready for a walk before you have even told him!

Teaching and learning

Your dog does not naturally know how to behave in our human world and it is up to you to show him. This will allow him to be a confident family pet who knows how to act in your home. You should always help your dog learn successfully, so you can reward his good behaviour.

BEHAVIOUR ADVICE LINE

How dogs learn

Dogs learn by seeing which behaviours are rewarded and which are not. If they behave in a way that is rewarded with praise or a treat, they will repeat it. If they behave in a way that doesn't get this response, they will try other behaviours until they find one that does. For example, by ignoring your dog when he jumps up to greet you, he will learn there is no point in doing it. But if he is rewarded for giving you a 'sit down hello', he will learn to behave that way. When teaching your dog to do something, do it in a quiet area and be ready to praise and reward him with treats.

Dogs should be discouraged from jumping up.

Shut the door

Try teaching your dog a trick like shutting the door, to build a bond with him.

1 Rub some sausage on a sticker so it smells nice.

2 Hold the sticker out to your dog and reward him when he sniffs it. Repeat, until he is doing this successfully.

3 Put the sticker on an open door and encourage your dog to nudge it shut. Reward him when he does this.

4 Start to say "shut it" just before he nudges the sticker, and then reward him.

5 Once he gets the idea, start to make the sticker smaller and smaller, until there is no sticker at all!

Top tip! If your dog doesn't understand what you are trying to teach him, take a little break. Then try making the task easier when you come back.

Ask the expert!

Q

Should I ever tell my dog off?

A

No. Your dog won't understand that you are telling him off because he has done something wrong. Instead, he may get nervous around you. It is better to ignore his bad behaviour and reward his good behaviour.

Chapter 6: Socialisation and training

🐾 First steps in socialisation

Puppies need to be introduced to people, animals and the outside world when they are young. This helps them become friendly and confident adults. The more your dog experiences as a puppy, the better off he will be. This process is called 'socialisation'.

Introduce family and friends as soon as possible.

Don't delay

It is best to socialise your dog as much as possible before he reaches 14 weeks. During this time, your puppy should be introduced to as many things as possible that he will encounter as an adult. If your puppy has not finished his vaccinations yet (see pages 52–53) ask your vet for advice on how to socialise him. You may be able to carry him into the outside world in your arms, for example.

It is also important to invite lots of different people to your house to visit. If they can bring their vaccinated dogs too, then it is even better. Make every encounter a happy and relaxed experience for your puppy. Stay relaxed yourself and encourage your puppy throughout.

Socialisation programme

This is a list of some common things to introduce your puppy to. Add some things from your local area, such as sheep and tractors if you live in the countryside. Allow your puppy to explore things in his own time and space, wherever possible. Calmly put some distance between your puppy and any situation he is not enjoying.

People
- People of different heights and sizes
- People with beards and moustaches
- People wearing hats and helmets
- People of different ages
- People on bikes, skateboards and in wheelchairs

Household items
- Vacuum cleaners
- Telephones
- Doorbells
- Televisions and stereos
- Lawn mowers
- Washing machines and tumble dryers

Outside noise
- Parks
- School grounds
- Fireworks
- Building sites
- Rivers, or the sea

Transport
- Trains
- Buses
- Motorcycles
- Cars
- Emergency vehicles
- Busy roads

Animals
- All kinds of dogs
- Cats
- Birds
- Horses
- Squirrels

Top tip! Get your dog used to loud noises such as trains, by playing them to him at a low volume first. You can find most of the sounds on the Internet.

 House training

Dogs prefer to go to the toilet away from their beds. It is up to you to train your dog to go to the toilet outside, away from the house. You should start housetraining your new dog as soon as you bring him home. Even if your dog is already housetrained, give him a refresher course.

Getting started

Begin housetraining by taking your dog to the same spot outside. Take your dog out first thing in the morning, after naps, exercise and meals and last thing at night. Puppies need to go out even more regularly – every 1–2 hours at first. Learn to predict when your dog needs to go to the toilet. A dog fidgeting, circling, squatting or sniffing are tell-tale signs. When this happens, encourage him to the door and follow these housetraining steps:

Simple housetraining

1 Take your dog out of the same door to the same place outside.

2 Once outside, wait with your dog and encourage him. Use a phrase to train him, such as "go toilet". Praise your dog when he's been and give him a treat.

3 Afterwards, spend a few minutes outside with your dog. This stops him delaying going to the toilet to spend more time with you.

4 If your dog does not go after a short while, take him back inside and watch closely in case he changes his mind.

Accidents

All dogs have accidents inside from time to time. If this happens do not get angry with your dog. It is best to clean the mess up when he's not even in the room. Your dog will not understand you are angry about the accident, only that you are angry. This will make him scared of you.

🐾 Basic training

You can begin the important task of training your dog as soon as you get him. Start with the basic training words "sit", "down" and "come here". Keep your training sessions short, simple and fun, with lots of encouragement and rewards.

Top tip!

Choose special dog treats that are soft and strong-smelling.

Sit

This is a simple and easy one for your dog to learn. Practise asking your dog to sit before giving him attention, food, or putting on his lead for a walk.

1 Hold a treat in front of his nose.

2 Move the treat up and back, so his bottom goes to sit down.

Once your dog has successfully learned Steps 1 and 2, say the word "sit" before you hold the treat in front of his nose.

Down

This is a trickier exercise, which will require some patience. Try teaching it just before a meal so your dog will be even keener for a treat.

1 While your dog is sitting, hold a treat next to his nose and lower it down between his paws.

2 Wait until your dog's head has come down to the ground and he stretches his front legs out, while you move your hand backwards.

Once your dog has successfully learned Steps 1 and 2, say the word "down" before you hold the treat next to his nose.

Come here

The trick with this game is for your dog to think you are more exciting than anything else. You will need his favourite toys and treats and an adult.

1 Have an adult hold your dog's collar as you show him a tasty treat and his favourite toy.

2 Move away from him.

3 Call "come here" and have the adult let go of your dog's collar.

4 As he runs to you, praise him and let him have the treat or a game with the toy.

🐾 Leads and walks

Your dog will need daily walks throughout his life to keep him fit, healthy and mentally stimulated. When walking your dog, there are places he will need to be on a lead (see page 62). Before taking your dog out for the first time, get him used to the lead with some training exercises in your garden.

Pulling on the lead

When walking on a lead, your dog will automatically want to pull you along. You have to teach your dog that pulling makes you stop, not go forward. Once he understands this, he will walk nicely on a loose lead and not rush off to explore things. But whenever the lead becomes taut, stop and don't move, so your dog understands pulling will get him nowhere. It often takes time to train your dog to walk on a loose lead, so keep your training sessions short and regular. You can also use a harness on your dog when you aren't going to do lead training.

Walking on a loose lead

1 Clip a lead onto your dog's collar.

2 Stand next to your dog and show him you have a treat.

3 Lift the treat up to your shoulder so that your dog looks up at you.

Top tip!

By law it is your job to clean up your dog's poo. Keep a supply of plastic bags with you to pick up the poo. Put the bag inside-out over your hand to pick up the poo. Make sure you dispose of the poo in special 'dog waste' bins, or at home.

4 Ask your dog to walk to "heel" and take a few steps forward.

5 As your dog walks forward with you, reward him by bringing your hand and the treat alongside your leg.

6 If your dog pulls forward, stand still and wait for him to come back to you before moving again.

Chapter 7: Grooming and health care

🐾 Grooming

Grooming is an important part of caring for your dog. It keeps him clean, healthy and looking good. It also teaches your dog that you will be handling him on a regular basis. Once your dog gets used to being groomed, it can be a bonding moment that brings you closer together. Make sure there is always an adult present when you do any of these grooming activities.

Inspecting

An important part of grooming your dog is inspecting his paws, ears and eyes.

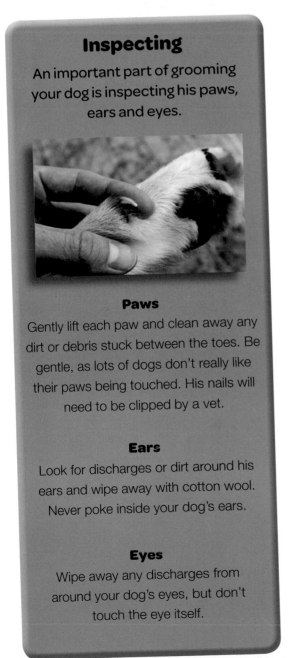

Paws

Gently lift each paw and clean away any dirt or debris stuck between the toes. Be gentle, as lots of dogs don't really like their paws being touched. His nails will need to be clipped by a vet.

Ears

Look for discharges or dirt around his ears and wipe away with cotton wool. Never poke inside your dog's ears.

Eyes

Wipe away any discharges from around your dog's eyes, but don't touch the eye itself.

Brushing

Regular brushing is the best way of looking after your dog's coat. It removes dirt, loose hair and dead skin, and stops the fur from becoming matted and tangled. Start brushing your dog while he is still a puppy with short sessions of 5–10 minutes. Shorthaired dogs should be brushed once a week, and longhaired dogs every day. When a dog is moulting, or shedding his hair, he will need to be brushed more often. Always have treats on hand to help your dog relax during a grooming session.

Brushing your dog

1 Sit or stand your dog outside or over some newspaper to catch dirt and loose hair.

2 Gently brush the hair over your dog's back in the direction it grows.

3 Brush the fur along your dog's belly and his ears, legs, head and tail.

Brushes

Use a bristle brush for short-haired dogs.

A pin brush is best for long-haired dogs.

A slicker brush removes loose hairs.

Baths

Dogs naturally keep their fur clean by licking it. Normally any dirt missed by your dog can be brushed away during grooming. However, when your dog has rolled in something particularly dirty or smelly, a bath is the only solution. Use lukewarm water and special dog shampoo to bathe your dog.

Teeth

Teeth-cleaning is an unusual experience for dogs to start with. Use water, dog toothpaste and a medium toothbrush to brush with. Keep daily teeth-cleaning sessions short and talk to your dog in a soothing voice as you brush.

🐾 Vaccinating and neutering

Within the first few days of getting your puppy, you will need to take him to a vet. The vet will check that your dog is healthy and book in a series of vaccination injections if he has not yet been vaccinated. These protect your dog against disease and mean that he can meet other animals outside your home.

Vaccination

Vaccination injections prevent your dog catching infectious diseases from other animals. The first round of vaccinations are given between 6 and 12 weeks of age, and the final round between 12 and 16 weeks of age. It is important that your dog is not let outside around any new animals until he has been adequately vaccinated. Your vet will take charge of your dog's injections and tell you when it is safe for him to go outside. Your vet will also book your dog in for booster injections around 12 months later.

Most injections are given in the scruff of the neck. Your dog is likely to feel nervous. Talk to him in a soothing voice throughout the injections and make sure you stay calm. If your dog senses you are anxious, he will become anxious too.

Neutering

While you are at the vet's it is important to discuss having your dog neutered. Neutering is a common operation that stops your dog becoming the parent to puppies. It is recommended that you have your dog neutered. Speak to your vet to decide when the best time to neuter is as this will depend on the individual dog.

Neutering can prevent many diseases in dogs and stops females trying to escape when they are 'in season'. It also prevents more dogs being brought into the world, when there are already too many dogs without homes.

Top tip!

If you have bought your dog from a breeder then he may have already had some vaccinations. If so, make sure the breeder gives you written details of which vaccinations he has received to show your vet.

Ask the expert!

Q

How often should my dog visit the vet?

A

Take your dog to the vet at least once a year for an annual check up.

🐾 Dog ailments

Dogs are strong, generally healthy creatures normally full of excitement, energy and enthusiasm. But, like humans, they also get sick from time to time. When this happens, your dog may display some tell-tale symptoms that let you know it is time to visit the vet.

Common ailments

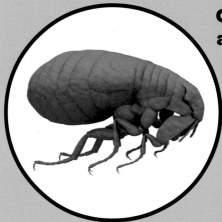

Fleas

Fleas are tiny, biting insects that live in your dog's coat and which can make him itch like crazy. Ask your vet for the best treatment.

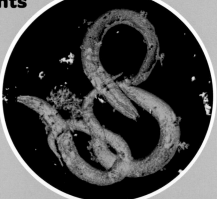

Worms

Worms are parasites that live inside your dog. Some come out like white noodles in your dog's poo. Dogs should be regularly treated for worms, even if there are no symptoms. Ask your vet about the best worm treatments.

What to look out for

A change in your dog's behaviour is often a sign he is unwell. He may be less hungry, become overly tired or uninterested in play. He could have bloodshot eyes, a discharge from his nose, a scruffy-looking coat, or he may be vomiting or have diarrhoea. If your dog's symptoms persist, it is best to contact your vet for advice. While you wait for your appointment, keep your dog in a quiet, warm place where he can rest.

Ask the expert!

Q

What should I do if my dog vomits?

A

It is not uncommon for a dog to vomit or get diarrhoea. If these symptoms continue for more than a day then take him to the vet.

Lice

Lice are biting insects like fleas, but white instead of reddish black. You will need to buy special shampoo from your vet if your dog has lice.

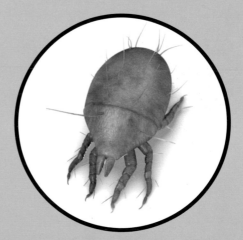

Ear mites

Mites live in your dog's ears and can cause itching, or a discharge. Visit the vet immediately if your dog displays these symptoms.

Chapter 8: Holidays

🐾 Holiday options

If you go on holiday without your dog you will need somebody to look after him. They will have to provide him with food, water, exercise and company. You could either leave your dog with a boarding kennel, responsible friends and family or a professional pet sitter.

Boarding kennels

Your dog can stay at a boarding kennel if he has had the relevant vaccinations (see pages 52–53). Your vet will be able to recommend a good kennel that provides individual sleeping quarters, a social dog area and a place he is walked. Ask for a tour of the kennel first and ask questions about how they will care for your dog.

A stay at a kennel can be great fun for your dog.

Ask the expert!

Q

How do I know if my dog enjoyed his boarding kennel?

A

Try a one-night stay at a kennel before the holiday. Your dog should come back happy and calm and like he has had a holiday himself!

Friends, family and neighbours

Make sure your dog has met his temporary carers beforehand. A walk with you and your dog is a great way to get used to new people. Add their address to your dog's identity tag and make sure they have emergency phone numbers for you and your vet. Don't forget your dog's bed, toys and of course his food!

Pet sitter

A pet sitter looks after your dog in your home, or has him to stay in theirs. It is best to meet the pet sitter first to discuss your dog's needs. A good pet sitter will ask about your dog's diet, his normal exercise routine, and what he likes and dislikes.

Travelling by car

If your dog is travelling with you, make sure he has regular toilet stops. Taking his blanket to lie on and a favourite toy can help with the journey. Remember never to leave your dog alone in a car.

Chapter 9: Getting older

🐾 Ageing dog care and saying goodbye

With proper exercise, a balanced diet, and loving owners, dogs are living longer than ever before. Depending on their size, breed or type, dogs often live to between 9 and 13 years of age. Older dogs often need extra care and attention as their needs change.

Caring for an elderly dog

As dogs get older they may slow down and become less active. As a result, they often put on weight. This can lead to obesity and brings with it serious health problems for your dog. To prevent this, feed your dog two to three smaller meals a day and weigh him regularly. Make sure you also exercise your older dog with frequent short walks instead of one long one. Let your dog set the pace and don't overtire him. The following checklist provides tips for caring for your dog in his old age.

Ageing dog care checklist

1 Brush his coat more often.

2 Make sure he has soft, warm, supportive bedding.

3 Go for at least two short walks a day.

4 Provide smaller meals that contain less fat.

Saying goodbye

Often dogs die naturally, but at other times disease and illness cause them to suffer. Sometimes, when a dog is in pain and has reached his last days, the kindest thing is to let the vet end his life with an injection. Your vet can help you decide what to do with your dog's remains, and often special caskets can be bought to bury him at home (see page 62).

Saying goodbye to a pet is like losing a member of the family and it helps to look at photos and talk about your fun times together. The main thing to remember is that you loved your dog and gave him a happy life.

Ask the expert!

Q

How long is a 'dog year'?

A

Traditionally, one dog year equals seven human years. But by today's standards, one dog year is considered to be between 5 and 6 human years. Smaller dogs usually live for longer than bigger dogs.

Top tip!

An old dog may become confused when he gets older and sometimes bark for no reason. Make sure you stay patient and calm with him at all times.

🐾 Glossary

Allergy
A physical reaction to something that doesn't agree with the body, such as dog hair.

Commitment
An ongoing obligation to carry something out.

Companion
A person or animal one spends a lot of time with.

Competitive
A desire to win.

Cross-breed
A dog bred from two different breeds.

Desirable
Wished for.

Diarrhoea
Explosive, runny poo.

Dog farmers
People who breed dogs for profit with no concern for their health, safety or welfare.

Housetrained
Trained to go to the toilet outside of the house.

Mental stimulation
Exercising the brain.

Microchipped
Inserting a microchip containing a special reference number into the scruff of a dog's neck. The microchip can be scanned to access the owner's details from a database.

Mongrel
A dog with parents from multiple breeds.

Moulting
Shedding hair to make way
for new hair growth.

Neutering
An operation that stops an
animal from having babies.

Parasite
A tiny creature that lives in
or on a bigger creature.

Playpen
A gated enclosure, to keep pets in.

Pure-breed
A dog bred from parents
of the same breed.

Roam
Move about over a wide area.

Social
Likes being around people
or animals.

Socialisation
The process of introducing
a dog to people and animals, so
he becomes used to them.

Titbits
Small pieces of tasty food.

Vaccination
A treatment to protect
against disease.

Vital
Absolutely necessary.

Worms
A parasite that lives in a
creature's stomach.

🐾 Dogs and the law

In the United Kingdom there are certain responsibilities that dog owners have to follow by law. These are set out below.

Duty of care

Under the law you must provide your dog with the following:

- A suitable environment.
- A suitable diet.
- Protection from pain, suffering, injury, disease, fear and distress.
- Freedom to express normal behaviours.

Dog burials

If you plan to bury your dog's remains in your garden, you will have to check your local council's regulations.

Local council information can be found at:

www.gov.uk/find-your-local-council

Dog identification

Under the law your dog must wear a collar and tag when it is in public. Your dog's tag must have your surname, telephone number, first line of your address and postcode. Check your local council's website for details of where your dog has to be on a lead and where he can be let off. From 2016, all dogs in England will have to be microchipped. Your vet or your local council can microchip your dog. See the Battersea Dogs & Cats Home website for more information on microchipping (see page 63 for website information).

Pet passports

Your dog can travel between the United Kingdom and certain other countries with a pet passport. If going abroad with your pet, plan in advance and check the following government website for up-to-date guidelines on requirements.

www.gov.uk/defra

Laws in other countries may be different so research the particular country's government website before you go. An Official Veterinarian (OV) can issue you with a dog passport. More information on pet passports and how to transport your dog overseas can be found at:

www.gov.uk/pet-travel-information-for-pet-owners

Top tip! Pet insurance is highly recommended to make sure the cost of your vet bills are covered. For further advice on this visit **battersea.org.uk**.

Index

About Battersea Dogs & Cats Home

Battersea Dogs & Cats Home looks after 6,000 dogs and 3,000 cats every year and is one of the oldest and most famous rescue centres in the world. We have been caring for lost, unwanted and neglected animals since 1860. We have three centres, at Battersea in London, at Old Windsor in Berkshire and at Brands Hatch in Kent. We aim never to turn away an animal in need, and our carers, vets, nurses and over 1,000 volunteers make sure all our residents are cared for while we try to find them loving new homes. Visit our website at **battersea.org.uk** to find out more about us.